THE SUNDIAL

GILLIAN CLARKE

Gillian Clarke

GOMER PRESS
1978

First Impression —May 1978

ISBN 0 85088 540 X

Printed by J. D. Lewis and Sons Ltd., Gomer Press, Llandysul

i

CATRIN, OWAIN a DYLAN

This volume is published
with the support of the
Welsh Arts Council

CONTENTS

ACKNOWLEDGEMENTS

Christopher Davies Limited (*Snow on the Mountain*)
Gwasg Gomer
Carcanet Press
Faber & Faber
Poetry Wales
The Anglo-Welsh Review
Aquarius
P.E.N. anthology
The Poetry Book Society Christmas Supplement, 1975
Spirit (U.S.A.)
Bardsides (U.S.A.)
B.B.C. Radio 3
B.B.C. Radio 4
Argo Records

THE SUNDIAL

Owain was ill today. In the night
He was delirious, shouting of lions
In the sleepless heat. Today, dry
And pale, he took a paper circle,
Laid it on the grass which held it
With curling fingers. In the still
Centre he pushed the broken bean
Stick, gathering twelve fragments
Of stone, placed them at measured
Distances. Then he crouched, slightly
Trembling with fever, calculating
The mathematics of sunshine.

He looked up, his eyes dark,
Intelligently adult as though
The wave of fever taught silence
And immobility for the first time.
Here, in his enforced rest, he found
Deliberation, and the slow finger
Of light, quieter than night lions,
More worthy of his concentration.
All day he told the time to me.
All day we felt and watched the sun
Caged in its white diurnal heat,
Pointing at us with its black stick.

JOURNEY

As far as I am concerned
We are driving into oblivion.
On either side there is nothing,
And beyond your driving
Shaft of light it is black.
You are a miner digging
For a future, a mineral
Relationship in the dark.
I can hear the darkness drip
From the other world where people
Might be sleeping, might be alive.

Certainly there are white
Gates with churns waiting
For morning, their cream standing.
Once we saw an old table
Standing square on the grass verge.
Our lamps swept it clean, shook
The crumbs into the hedge and left it.
A tractor too, beside a load
Of logs, bringing from a deeper
Dark a damp whiff of the fungoid
Sterility of the conifers.

Complacently I sit, swathed
In sleepiness. A door shuts
At the end of a dark corridor.
Ahead not a cat's eye winks
To deceive us with its green
Invitation. As you hurl us
Into the black contracting
Chasm, I submit like a blind
And folded baby, being born.

LUNCHTIME LECTURE

And this from the second or third millenium
B.C., a female, aged about twenty-two.
A white, fine skull, full up with darkness
As a shell with sea, drowned in the centuries.
Small, perfect. The cranium would fit the palm
Of a man's hand. Some plague or violence
Destroyed her, and her whiteness lay safe in a shroud
Of silence, undisturbed, unrained on, dark
For four thousand years. Till a tractor in summer
Biting its way through the longcairn for supplies
Of stone, broke open the grave and let a crowd of light
Stare in at her, and she stared quietly back.

As I look at her I feel none of the shock
The farmer felt as, unprepared, he found her.
Here in the Museum, like death in hospital,
Reasons are given, labels, causes, catalogues.
The smell of death is done. Left, only her bone
Purity, the light and shade beauty that her man
Was denied sight of, the perfect edge of the place
Where the pieces join, with no mistakes, like boundaries.

She's a tree in winter, stripped white on a black sky,
Leafless formality, brow, bough in fine relief.
I, at some other season, illustrate the tree
Fleshed, with woman's hair and colours and the rustling
Blood, the troubled mind that she has overthrown.
We stare at each other, dark into sightless
Dark, seeing only ourselves in the black pools,
Gulping the risen sea that booms in the shell.

DEATH OF A YOUNG WOMAN

She died on a hot day. In a way
Nothing was different. The stretched white
Sheet of her skin tightened no further.
She was fragile as a yacht before,
Floating so still on the blue day's length,
That one would not know when the breath
Blew out and the sail finally slackened.
Her eyes had looked opaquely in the
Wrong place to find those who smiled
From the bedside, and for a long time
Our conversations were silent.

The difference was that in her house
The people were broken by her loss.
He wept for her and for the hard tasks
He had lovingly done, for the short,
Fierce life she had lived in the white bed,
For the burden he had put down for good.
As we sat huddled in pubs supporting
Him with beer and words' warm breath,
We felt the hollowness of his release.
Our own ungrateful health prowled, young,
Gauche about her death. He was polite,
Isolated. Free. No point in going home.

BLAEN CWRT

You ask how it is. I will tell you.
There is no glass. The air spins in
The stone rectangle. We warm our hands
With apple wood. Some of the smoke
Rises against the ploughed, brown field
As a sign to our neighbours in the
Four folds of the valley that we are in.
Some of the smoke seeps through the stones
Into the barn where it curls like fern
On the walls. Holding a thick root
I press my bucket through the surface
Of the water, lift it brimming and skim
The leaves away. Our fingers curl on
Enamel mugs of tea, like ploughmen.
The stones clear in the rain
Giving their colours. It's not easy.
There are no brochure blues or boiled sweet
Reds. All is ochre and earth and cloud-green
Nettles tasting sour and the smells of moist
Earth and sheep's wool. The wattle and daub
Chimney hood has decayed away, slowly
Creeping to dust, chalking the slate
Floor with stories. It has all the first
Necessities for a high standard
Of civilised living : silence inside
A circle of sound, water and fire,
Light on uncountable miles of mountain
From a big, unpredictable sky,
Two rooms, waking and sleeping,
Two languages, two centuries of past
To ponder on, and the basic need
To work hard in order to survive.

CATRIN

I can remember you, child,
As I stood in a hot, white
Room at the window watching
The people and cars taking
Turn at the traffic lights.
I can remember you, our first
Fierce confrontation, the tight
Red rope of love which we both
Fought over. It was a square
Environmental blank, disinfected
Of paintings or toys. I wrote
All over the walls with my
Words, coloured the clean squares
With the wild, tender circles
Of our struggle to become
Separate. We want, we shouted,
To be two, to be ourselves.

Neither won nor lost the struggle
In the glass tank clouded with feelings
Which changed us both. Still I am fighting
You off, as you stand there
With your straight, strong, long
Brown hair and your rosy,
Defiant glare, bringing up
From the heart's pool that old rope,
Tightening about my life,
Trailing love and conflict,
As you ask may you skate
In the dark, for one more hour.

SNOW ON THE MOUNTAIN

There was a girl riding a white pony
Which seemed an elemental part
Of the snow. A crow cut a clean line
Across the hill, which we grasped as a rope
To pull us up the pale diagonal.

The point was to be first at the top
Of the mountain. Our laughter bounced far
Below us like five fists full of pebbles. About us
Lay the snow, deep in the hollows,
Very clean and dry, untouched.

I arrived breathless, my head breaking
The surface of the glittering light, thinking
No place could claim more beauty, white
Slag tips like cones of sugar spun
By the pit wheels under Machen mountain.

I sat on a rock in the sun, watching
My snowboys play. Pit villages shine
Like anthracite. Completed, the pale rider
Rode away. I turned to him, and saw
His joy fall like the laughter down a dark
Crack. The black crow shadowed him.

THE FOX

On the way we saw the red larch woods
Blurring the mountain above Llwyn Onn,
Two hills, one rising, intensely warm with colour,
One flying free and horizontal from the plane of symmetry.

Those foxwood reds were still warm in the brain
When we walked from Blaen Cwrt across the fields
To the south side of the hill, under the oak wood,
Where the ewes shelter to give birth to their lambs.

The floor of the wood glimmered with white bones ;
Little, silver skulls eyed us darkly, and the lambs
Leapt away round the hill. The blood of birth
And life stained the pale bones of the past.

Violence brushed our faces when we found
The vixen hanging from a tree. She was shot.
Her beautiful head thrown back, her life stiffened,
Her milk dry, her fertility frozen. The reds grew cold.

COMMUNITY

We talk, especially at night
When we light fires and eat together.
I know my job, they know theirs.
We came here at random, drawn
By the place, related by love
Running like a fine metal
Chain through assorted beads
Forming between this and the next
A separate relationship.
One can stand aside and watch
The spatial movement, understanding
Edge forward, falter and change
Form. Or one can move in and feel space
Contract, aware of an approach.

I lay the plates on the table,
One before each, each one evidence
Of my concern for the man or child
Who pulls forward a chair and eats.
Our eyes sting in the smoky room.
We are tired early and take our turn
At the light of the fire to wash.
I hang down my hair to brush it.
In the little house at night
We can hear each other breathe,
Turning in our beds, and things
Moving in the grass, and the leaves
Of the laburnum trees combing
The roof all night.

DYDDGU REPLIES TO DAFYDD

All year in open places, underneath
   the frescoed forest ceiling,
   we have made ceremony
   out of this seasonal love.

Dividing the leaf-shade as divers white
   in green pools we rose to dry
   islands of sudden sun. Then
   love seemed generosity.

Original sin I whitened from your
   mind, my colours influenced
   your flesh, as sun on the floor
   and warm furniture of a church.

So did our season bloom in mild weather,
   reflected gold like butter
   under chins, repeatedly
   unfolding to its clock of seed.

Autumn, our forest room is growing cold.
   I wait, shivering, feeling a
   dropping sun, a coming dark,
   your heart changing the subject.

The season coughs as it falls, like a coal ;
   the trees ache. The forest falls
   to ruin, a roofless minister
   where only two still worship.

Love still, like sun, a vestment, celebrates,
   its warmth about our shoulders.
   I dread the day when Dyddgu's once
   loved name becomes a common cloak.

Your touch is not so light. I grow heavy.
   I wait too long, grow anxious,
   note your changing gestures, fear
   desire's alteration.

The winter stars are flying and the owls
   sing. You are packing your songs
   in a sack, narrowing your
   words, as you stare at the road.

The feet of young men beat, somewhere far off
   on the mountain. I would women
   had roads to tread in winter
   and other lovers waiting.

A raging rose all summer falls to snow,
   keeping its continuance in
   frozen soil. I must be patient
   for the breaking of the crust.

I must be patient that you will return
   when the wind whitens the tender
   underbelly of the March grass
   thick as pillows under the oaks.

Dyddgu is the woman to whom the medieval Welsh poet,
Dafydd ap Gwilym, addressed many of his love poems.

AT YSTRAD FFLUR

No way of flowers at this late season.
   Only a river blossoming on stone
   and the mountain ash in fruit.

All rivers are young in these wooded hills
   where the abbey watches and the young Teifi
   counts her rosary on stones.

I cross by a simple bridge constructed
   of three slim trees. Two lie across. The third
   is a broken balustrade.

The sun is warm after rain on the red
   pelt of the slope, fragmentary through trees
   like torches in the dark.

They have been here before me and have seen
   the sun's lunulae in the profound
   quietness of water.

The Teifi is in full flood and rich
   with metals : a torc in a brown pool
   gleaming for centuries.

I am spellbound in a place of spells. Cloud
   changes gold to stone as their circled bones
   dissolve in risen corn.

The river races for the south too full
   of summer rain for safety, spilt water
   whitening low-lying fields.

From oak and birchwoods through the turning **trees**
    where leaf and hour and century fall
    seasonally, desire runs

    Like sparks in stubble through the memory
      of the place, and a yellow mustard field
      is a sheet of flame in the heart.

The medieval Welsh love poet, Dafydd ap Gwilym, was
buried at Ystrad Fflur.

SWINGING

At the end of the hot day it rains
Softly, stirring the smells from the raked
Soil. In her sundress and shorts she rocks
On the swing, watching the rain run down
Her brown arms, hands folded warm between
Small thighs, watching her white daps darken
And soak in the cut and sodden grass.

She used to fling her anguish into
My arms, staining my solitude with
Her salt and grimy griefs. Older now
She runs, her violence prevailing
Against silence and the avenue's
Complacency, I her hatred's object.

Her dress, the washed green of deck chairs, sun
Bleached and chalk-sea rinsed, colours the drops,
And her hair a flag, half and then full
Mast in the apple-trees, flies in the face
Of the rain. Raised now her hands grip tight
The iron rods, her legs thrusting the tide
Of rain aside until, parallel
With the sky, she triumphs and gently
Falls. A green kite. I wind in the string.

SHEEP'S SKULLS

The bone is thin as paper
Inside the skull, scrolled on shadow.
Its dreams evaporated
On a warm bank over the drover's road
To Capel Cynon.

We sought skulls like mushrooms,
Uncertainly white at a distance,
Skulls of sheep, rabbit, bird,
Beautiful as a leaf's skeleton
Or derelict shell,

Where sheep shelter inside stone
Cottages, graze the floors clean, stare
From the window spaces. They die
On the open hill, and raven and buzzard
Come like women to clean them.

The skull's caves are secretive.
The crazed bone, sometimes translucent
As vellum, sometimes shawled
To lace, no longer knocks with the heart's bell
To the lamb in the womb.

A spider wraps it in a tress
Of silk, a cloth of light. On the rose
Patina of old wood it lies
Ornamental in the reflection
Of a jar of wheat stalks.

BABY-SITTING

I am sitting in a strange room listening
For the wrong baby. I don't love
This baby. She is sleeping a snuffly
Roseate, bubbling sleep ; she is fair ;
She is a perfectly acceptable child.
I am afraid of her. If she wakes
She will hate me. She will shout
Her hot, midnight rage, her nose
Will stream disgustingly and the perfume
Of her breath will fail to enchant me.

To her I will represent absolute
Abandonment. For her it will be worse
Than for the lover cold in lonely
Sheets ; worse than for the woman who waits
A moment to collect her dignity
Beside the bleached bone in the terminal ward.
As she rises sobbing from the monstrous land
Stretching for milk-familiar comforting,
She will find me and between us two
It will not come. It will not come.

IN PISGAH GRAVEYARD

Dylan tells me this is a church-garden.
Indeed, these bones, ground seed-small, seem neither
Static nor dead. The flowers that flourish
Here suggest fertility, the seed-heads
Of late summer brave, casting away
Their foliage, the naked sky. *Er côf*
On every stone, I count the time each
One was allowed, arrange their families,
Imagined, in the old farms and places
That watch still from the mountains.

The warmth tumbles here like a giant sun
Flower dying and full of glossy seed.
This roughest stone of all, a sand-stone pod
Bursting with words, is Dewi Emrys's grave.
And all around the living corn concedes
Fecundity to him. They're proud of him
Here, where full barns count as much as poetry.
He who, they say, knew women as well as words,
Lies in the blond fields blowing to seed
With the threshing machine and the chapel clock.

What do I look for here, with a child's
Hot hand in mine, his hair like ragged robin ?
Perhaps the stone words of my first tongue
On a poet's grave that tidies his wild life,
For the savage roar of the trapped sun
Seeding the earth against the stop of winter
When everything that lives will play dead lions,
And the flaming mane of the surrounding wheat
Drops down, lies still until, inside the heart,
The words unfreeze and the poems come again.

SAILING

It was very strange to watch him sail
Away from me on the calm water,
The white sail duplicate. I knew
All the people in the boat and felt
The tightening lines of my involvement.

My children were in the boat, and my friends,
And he in the stern. The sheet of water
Thinned between us as he sailed away.
I strolled on the path and waved
And felt in the space a terrible desolation.

When they returned the exhilaration
Of the familiar morning had gone. I felt
As though on the water he had found
New ways of evasion, a sheet
Of icy water to roll out between us.

BIRTH

On the hottest, stillest day of the summer
A calf was born in a field
At Pant-y-Cetris ; two buzzards
Measured the volume of the sky ;
The hills brimmed with incoming
Night. In the long grass we could see
The cow, her sides heaving, a focus
Of restlessness in the complete calm,
Her calling at odds with silence.

The light flowed out leaving stars
And clarity. Hot and slippery, the scalding
Baby came, and the cow stood up, her cool
Flanks like white flowers in the dark.
We waited while the calf struggled
To stand, moved as though this
Were the first time. I could feel the soft sucking
Of the new-born, the tugging pleasure
Of bruised reordering, the signal
Of milk's incoming tide, and satisfaction
Fall like a clean sheet around us.

RAILWAY TRACKS

When you talk to me of carrots fresh pulled
From your grandfather's allotment, how he
Would wash the soil away in the green rain
Of the water butt, and then shake them dry ;
When I see you carry your fruit away
To the railway bank, and feast there neck high
In golden, seeded grass and flowering weeds,
I see my own mysterious railway track,
Ragwort, dog daisies and valerian
Swim in the great heat on the waves of grass.
Sweet surreptitious smells, like tar and sweat,
And dusty arms, and pollen on my knees.
A vast, dead brick building with a hundred
Broken windows, the track losing its way
Besieged by leaf and stalk and flowerhead
Triumphant to be brought again to their
Own country. Above all, leaping from sleeper
To sleeper, along these lines that lead deep
And parallel into the wilderness,
I hear another footfall follow mine.

But who that child was, what the happiness,
And where the track, no one can tell me now.
It was as good as carrots on the bank
To find a place where wildness had returned.
The old, blind warehouse, full of swooping birds,
Has given me a taste for dereliction,
For the fall of towers, the rot of stone and brick,
For the riot of the ragged weed's return,
The reinstatement of the wilderness.

FOGHORNS

When Catrin was a small child
She thought the foghorn moaning
Far out at sea was the sad
Solitary voice of the moon
Journeying to England.
She heard it warn "Moon, Moon,"
As it worked the Channel, trading
Weather like rags and bones.

Tonight, after the still sun
And the silent heat, as haze
Became rain and weighed glistening
In brimful leaves, and the last bus
Splashes and fades with a soft
Wave-sound, the foghorns moan, moon-
Lonely and the dry lawns drink.
This dimmed moon, calling still,
Hauls sea-rags through the streets.

STORM AWST

The cat walks. It listens, as I do,
To the wind which leans its iron
Shoulders on our door. Neither
The purr of a cat nor my blood
Runs smoothly for elemental fear
Of the storm. This then is the big weather
They said was coming. All the signs
Were bad, the gulls coming in white,
Lapwings gathering, the sheep too
Calling all night. The gypsies
Were making their fires in the woods
Down there in the east . . . always
A warning. The rain stings, the whips
Of the laburnum hedge lash the roof
Of the cringing cottage. A curious
Calm, coming from the storm, unites
Us, as we wonder if the work
We have done will stand. Will the tyddyn
In its group of strong trees on the high
Hill, hold against the storm Awst
Running across hills where everything
Alive listens, pacing its house, heart still ?

storm Awst : August storm
tyddyn : smallholding

BEECH BUDS

The beech buds are breaking. I feel so happy.
I snapped the bare twigs in a wood
A month ago. I put them in a wine bottle
Filled with water, not for the twigs, for the light
Blown bubbles to float in the shine of the water.

It was like that with my life. I put
Something that was dead and bare into
The brightness of your love, not so that
Leaf would break, but for the bubbles
Of silver against the light. From the hard,
Brittle wood came tenderness and life, numerous
Damp, green butterflies, transparently veined,
Opening like a tree that is alive.

WATERFALL

We parked the car in a dusty village
That sat sideways on a hill over the coal.
We heard a rag-and-bone-man
And a curlew. The sun for the first time
Put a warm hand across our shoulders
And touched our winter faces.

We saw summer, one lapwing to go.
Her mate was in the sky already,
Turning over, black, white-bellied,
While she, looking browner near the ground,
Tidied the winter from her crisp field.

We climbed the mountain, crossed the round
Of it, following the marshland down to the gorge.
The water was gathering minutely everywhere
Knowing its place and its time were coming.

Down over the boulders in the death bed
Of an old river, through thin birches and oaks,
Going where the water went, into the multitude
Of the shouting streams, no longer speaking
To each other, silenced by what the water said.

Closer to crisis the air put cold silk
Against our faces and the cliffs streamed
With sun water, caging on every gilded
Ledge small things that flew by mistake
Into the dark spaces behind the rainbows.

The path led me under the fall to feel
The arc of the river and the mountain's exact
Weight ; the roar of rain and lapwings
Leaving ; water-beat, heart-fall in accord,
Curlew-call, child-cry on the drum's skin
Distinguished from the inmost thoughts of rivers.

We cage our response in the roar, defer
Decision while water falls. It gathers its life
On our behalf, leaps for us, its chords
Of change that curve across the cliffs
Are only, after all, an altering of level
To where it belongs, though the falling appals.

CURLEW

She dips her bill in the rim of the sea.
Her beak is the elipse
of a world much smaller
than that far section of the sea's
circumference. A curve enough to calculate
the field's circle and its heart
of eggs in the cold grass.

All day while I scythed my territory
out of nettles, laid claim to my cantref,
she has cut her share of sky. Her song bubbles
long as a plane trail from her savage mouth.
I clean the blade with newspaper. Dusk blurs
circle within circle till there's nothing left
but the egg pulsing in the dark against her ribs.
For each of us the possessed space contracts
to the nest's heat, the blood's small circuit.

CURLEWS

We crouched in the wet field, gambling
Numb hours for the prize of a curlew's
Nest. The pair fussed in the sky, diving
To run in the lost lanes of the grass.

We heard the young call close to us
In small mimicry of adult
Panic, flecked, soft spheres on long,
Grey legs, following the sky's signal.

We held one, folded and frail, beak
Minutely curved, freckled like a blown,
Pale dandelion. Then it ran, free,
Into the secret homeward corridors.

Our important morning had given
Its joy. Then we turned to go home
And found the broken baby curlew,
Death glazing its black eyes with pain.

Inconsolably we watched the head
Loll from the snapped stem of its neck
Like the hung clock of a dandelion
Wasting its seed. We grieved to see.

Time fall, life by life, no comfort to give
To each other. Did we crush it
As we passed, greedy as hunters
To possess the summer's wildness ?

STILL LIFE

It was good tonight
To polish brass with you,
Our hands slighty gritty
With Brasso, as they would feel
If we'd been in the sea, salty.
It was as if we burnished
Our friendship, polished it
Until all the light-drowning
Tarnish of deceit
Were stroked away. Patterns
Of incredible honesty
Delicately grew, revealed
Quite openly to the pressure
Of the soft, torn rag.
We made a yellow-gold
Still-life out of clocks,
Candlesticks and kettles.
My sadness puzzled you.
I rubbed the full curve
Of an Indian goblet,
Feeling its illusory
Heat. It cooled beneath
My fingers and I read
In the braille formality
Of pattern, in the leaf
And tendril and stylised tree,
That essentially each
Object remains cold,
Separate, only reflecting
The other's warmth.

ST. AUGUSTINE'S, PENARTH

The church is like the prow
Of a smoky ship, moving
On the down channel currents
To open sea. A stone

Figurehead, the flowing light
Streams from it. From everywhere
You can see Top Church, remote
As high church is from chapel.

Church high on the summit
Of the climbing town
Where I was a child, where rain
Runs always slantingly

On streets like tilted chutes
Of grey sliding on all sides
From the church, to sea and dock,
To shopping streets and home.

Breasting the cloud, its stone
Profile of an ancient priest
Preaches continuity
In the face of turning tides.

NIGHTRIDE

The road unwinding under our wheels
New in the headlamps like a roll of foil.
The rain is a recorder writing tunes
In telegraph wires, kerbs and cats' eyes,
Reflections and the lights of little towns.

He turns his head to look at me.
' Why are you quiet ? ' Shiny road rhythm,
Rain rhythm, beat of the windscreen wipers,
I push my knee against his in the warmth
And the car thrusts the dark and rain away.

The child sleeps, and I reflect, as I breathe
His brown hair, and watch the apple they gave him
Held in his hot hands, that a tree must ache
With the sweet weight of the round rosy fruit,
As I with Dylan's head, nodding on its stalk.

GOING AWAY

A chrysanthemum exploded
Silently, turning its small palm
Upwards in a spread gesture
Of personal hopelessness.

That was my first sight of the dark.
The rain rushed, making November
Windows into patterns as sad
As the Art Deco linoleum.

His hands on regulation sheets ;
They and his face lay calmly, three
Sallow blossoms on the white. We
Formed a familiar trinity.

Unable to bear a going
Away, I abandoned them both
That night, for fear of knowing
Precisely the difference death made.

Today there is again a dumb
Implosion spreading its violence
Soundlessly, muffled by flesh. Again
Separation reopens the void.

TWO WORKING

We worked silently. I became
Accustomed to the words spoken
Not to me, but to the tools
And stones which engrossed you.
I was the craftsman's mate, one
Who fetched wood and merged sometimes
My glance with yours, bringing food
And hot tea to you and comfort
When the cold, hard stones turned on you.

As I stood still and cold, holding
Things for you, I thought there can be
On the white page between two who work
Together a line that perfectly
Delineates the flint edge of land
And the spinning light of sky, once
Distinguishing and unifying
Two who work with stone just under
Where the curlew draws the sky line.

RETURN TO PENARTH

I lived here once, on the top floor
Of this steep town, all of its rooms
Windowed with grey sea. These houses
Keep their watch, old and half-blind,
Wall-eyed and white with premonitions
Of rain from England. The cliffs lift
Up their crumbling limestone hands
For the winds from the other coast
To unskein our grey tides neatly.

Then, on dark nights, the town seemed
Very old. Under my feet I felt
The shaking of the floors, the cliffs
Far down disintegrate before
The nudging tides. Over the stretched
Sea, tensing to crease at its rim,
The known cadence of the Breaksea
Lightship beats rhythm with the stars,
A pulse in bone, marking all time.

Now new white slabs shoulder the steep
Roofs of the town from the sky line.
The rocks release their fossils,
Their pink and white boulders, at the touch
Of the sea. The slag the rivers
Bring from the heartlands, works among
The ancient stones. The new blocks stare
To England, above the blue surface
Where fine reflected weather smoothes
Over the estuary's silt
Of inherited sadness. But
I can hear it when the tide breathes
In, and spits the grit out on the shore.

LINES

Diagonally the line
Dips between the trees
And the house. It wavers
Like the uncertain edge of a flag,
At the same time dividing
The space, charting one triangle
With clean white gestures,
And pegging together with small,
Desperate wooden teeth
The closed wound.

Ostensibly I lie
Sunbathing. I can feel
That wound of the divided
Mind : the upper triangle
Is rational. The aspens
Spinning leaves like florins
Up there in the light
Assert that it was good
For me, the pain.

        Below
In the other part the blind
Blue, polythene pool,
Trawling coins and the dark
Sides of aspen moons,
Holds but sees no light.
The laundered people drown
In my pool. They wave
Their fistless arms, irregular
As images in a hall
Of mirrors.

At the end
Of the day I stood up, shook
The kaleidoscope,
Watching the circles and flakes
Of light falling, and a red
Plastic steamer going
Nowhere, bumping the sides
Like a moth at a shut
Window. The shapes fell
In a coloured muddle on the grass.
Neatly, slowly I folded
Clothes, and survived.

TWO POINTS OF VIEW

The combine harvester has completed
Its traditionally squared field, a shawl
Dropped on the cliff. Because it is Sunday
The red machine stands still and powerful
As a ladybird resting between flight.

It is sad, you say, the yellow leaf
And the cut field, and the slow September
Sea balancing midlanders returning
Soon to their own black country.
You sit watching the tide recede, the stalks

Of the severed corn bleeding our summer
Life. I see Islwyn yesterday in the lane
Standing erect, straw-headed in the last
Load. I watch them reserve a proportion
Of the harvest for the resurrection.

BURNING NETTLES

Where water springs, pools, waits
Collection in a bucket
In the late summer heat,
Beech trees observe foresight
Of autumn wrinkling their leaves.
The cold will wither this
Old garden. The plumpness shrinks
Beneath its skin, a light
Frown puckers the mirrored sky.

The scythe bleeds ancient herbs
Whose odours come as ghosts
To disturb memory.
My fire of nettles crackles
Like bees creeping in a green
Hive, making white smoke from weeds,
And the strange, sweet plants Marged
Sowed, or Nanu, before
The wind changed from the east.

With the reaping hook blade
I lift an exhausted moth
From the hot mound. It lives
To die of cold. Inside the cave
Of thatched grass the secret fire
Thrives on my summer. Nettles
Turn to ashes in its heart,
Crucible of the fragrant and
The sour. Only soil survives.

Rose bay willowherb, ragwort,
Grass, disintegrate and make
A white continuous mane
For the mountain. Ponies turn
Windward. The evening's heat
Belies the beech tree's shiver,
And pinpoints of ice on skin
Are nettlestings, not rain. Fire,
Buried in flower-heads, makes
Bright ritual of decay,
Transubstantiates the green
Leaf to fertility.

HARVEST AT MYNACHLOG

At last the women come with baskets,
The older one in flowered apron,
A daisied cloth covering the bread
And dappled china, sweet tea
In a vast can. The women stoop
Spreading their cups in the clover.

The engines stop. A buzzard watches
From the fence. We bury our wounds
In the deep grass : sunburnt shoulders,
Bodies scratched with straw, wrists bruised
From the weight of the bales, blood beating.

For hours the baler has been moulding
Golden bricks from the spread straw,
Spewing them at random in the stubble.
I followed the slow load, heaved each
Hot burden, feeling the sun contained.

And unseen over me a man leaned,
Taking the weight to make the toppling
Load. Then the women came, friendly
And cool as patches of flowers at the far
Field edge, mothy and blurred in the heat.

We are soon recovered and roll over
In the grass to take our tea. We talk
Of other harvests. They remember
How a boy, flying his plane so low
Over the cut fields that his father

Straightened from his work to wave his hat
At the boasting sky, died minutes later
On an English cliff, in such a year
As this, the barns brimming gold.

We are quiet again, holding our cups
In turn for the tilting milk, sad, hearing
The sun roar like a rush of grain
Engulfing all winged things that live
One moment in the eclipsing light.

ST. THOMAS'S DAY

It's the darkest morning of the year.
Day breaks in water runnels
In the yard ; a flutter
Of light on a tiled roof ;
The loosening of night's
Stonehold on tap and bolt.

Rain on my face wakes me
From recent sleep. I cross
The yard, shovel bumping
In the barrow, fingers
Stiff as hinges. Catrin
Brings bran and fresh hay.

A snort in the dark, a shove
For supremacy.
My hands are warmed
In the steam of his welcome.
Midwinter, only here
Do the fields still summer,
Thistlehead and flower
Powdered by hoof and tooth.

LAST RITES

During this summer of the long drought
The road to Synod Inn has kept
Its stigmata of dust and barley seed ;

At the inquest they tell it again :
How the lorry tents us from the sun,
His pulse dangerous in my hands,
A mains hum only, no message
Coming through. His face warm, profiled
Against tarmac, the two-stroke Yamaha
Dead as a black horse in a war.
Only his hair moves and the sound
Of the parched grass and harebells a handspan
Away, his fear still with me like the scream
Of a jet in an empty sky.
I cover him with the grey blanket
From my bed, touch his face as a child
Who makes her favourites cosy.
His blood on my hands, his cariad in my arms.

Driving her home we share that vision
Over August fields dying of drought
Of the summer seas shattering
At every turn of Cardigan Bay
Under the cruel stones of the sun.

CLYWEDOG

The people came out in pairs.
Old, most of them, holding their places
Close till the very last minute,
Even planting the beans as usual
That year, grown at last accustomed
To the pulse of the bulldozers.
High in those uphill gardens, scarlet
Beanflowers blazed hours after
The water rose in the throats of the farms.

Only the rooted things stayed :
The wasted hay, the drowned
Dog roses, the farms, their kitchens silted
With their own stones, hedges
And walls a thousand years old.
And the mountains, in a head-collar
Of flood, observe a desolation
They'd grown used to before the coming
Of the wall-makers. Language
Crumbles to wind and bird-call.

IN DONEGAL

"There is blood on the sea."
Dylan insists.
But it is only the stain
Of a floating weed, hair

loosening on the lifting wave.
Our stones fall silently sheer
into bladderwrack. I feel
the sun strike and the sea beat

and remember Ynys Lochtyn
in the snow last winter, ponies
huddled in a cwtch of thorns, warm
in the snow of their own hair,

storm-herded. That night on the farm
they lay listening, alert,
uncertain of gunshot for the wind
and sleet and the dogs growling.

So nobody saw the ponies'
driven snow, the terrible fall
of a white wave breaking, the storm's
eye in the skull of a mare.

We watch the calm sea rising
and falling here off Donegal.
It is blue with hot summer, red
with bloodweed, too far below
our thrown stones to cry out.

CHOUGHS

I follow you downhill to the edge
My feet taking as naturally as yours
To a sideways tread, finding footholds
Easily in the turf, accustomed
As we are to a sloping country.

The cliffs buttress the bay's curve to the north
And here drop sheer and sudden to the sea.
The choughs plummet from sight then ride
The updraught of the cliffs' mild yellow
Light, fold, fall with closed wings from the sky.

At the last moment as in unison they turn
A ripcord of the wind is pulled in time.
He gives her food and the saliva
Of his red mouth, draws her black feathers, sweet
As shining grass across his bill.

Rare birds that pair for life. There they go
Divebombing the marbled wave a yard
Above the spray. Wings flick open
A stoop away
From the drawn teeth of the sea.